21st Century Skills Library

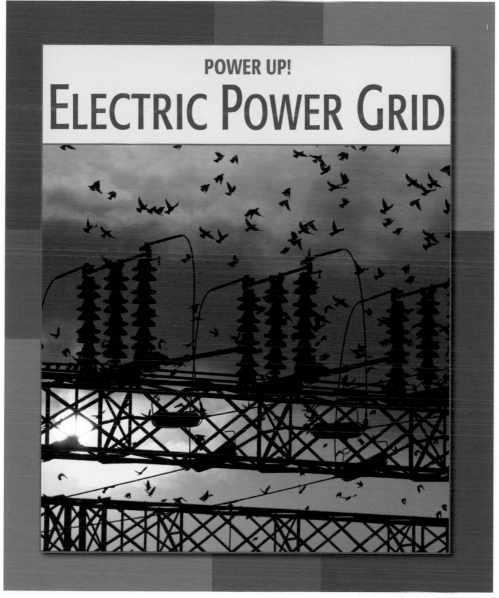

POWER UP!

ELECTRIC POWER GRID

Patricia Hynes

Cherry Lake Publishing
Ann Arbor, Michigan

Published in the United States of America by Cherry Lake Publishing
Ann Arbor, MI
www.cherrylakepublishing.com

Library of Congress Cataloging-in-Publication Data
Hynes, Patricia Freeland.
  The electric power grid/by Patricia Freeland Hynes.
      p. cm.—(Power up!)
  Includes bibliographical references and index.
  ISBN-13: 978-1-60279-042-1 (lib. bdg.)   978-1-60279-101-5 (pbk.)
  ISBN-10: 1-60279-042-6 (lib. bdg.)   1-60279-101-5 (pbk.)
  1. Electric power distribution—Juvenile literature. I. Title. II.
Series.
  TK3001.H96 2008
  621.319—dc22   2007005619

*Cherry Lake Publishing would like to acknowledge the work of
The Partnership for 21st Century Skills.
Please visit www.21stcenturyskills.org for more information.*

TABLE OF CONTENTS

CHAPTER ONE

Living Without Electricity

*Reading a book at night with the light of just a
single candle can be quite a challenge.*

Did you know that millions of people around the globe do not have

access to electricity? Tens of millions of others get electricity for just a

couple of hours a day. Over time, they've learned to "make do" in a

bad situation.

Only in the last hundred years have millions of other people come to rely on electricity. Before that, Americans and everybody else lit their homes with candles and read books or played cards for entertainment.

Today, American society cannot operate without electricity. It powers the clock radios that wake us up. It brews the morning coffee. It runs the lights in schools. It operates the elevators and escalators in office buildings.

But where does this electricity come from? How do we manufacture it, and how does it get to where it needs to go? This book is the story of the nationwide system that makes our lives possible.

Learning & Innovation Skills

American society has only been dependent upon electricity for less than 125 years. Before that, candles were the main source of light. Pretend we had to go back to "candle power." How would that change your life?

CHAPTER TWO

Blackout!

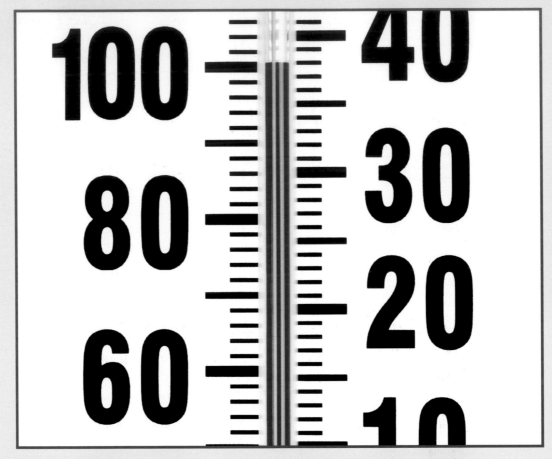

Heat waves often cause city mayors to declare emergencies and open "cooling centers" for citizens who do not have air conditioning.

"I t's at least 100 degrees out there," Jackson announced as he flopped on

the sofa in his family's New York apartment. His shirt was soaking wet.

"It's not safe to be running around in this heat and humidity, even for someone your age," Grandma said as she walked into the living room carrying a sweater. "Besides, you don't want to have to rush to the movies."

Mom eyed Grandma's sweater. "Do you think you'll need that?"

"I always get cold at the movies. The air conditioning . . ."

"Speaking of air conditioning," yelled older brother Jeff, "what's wrong with ours?" He sat hunched over his computer in his bedroom, working on a college history paper.

During weather extremes, many people rely on TV newscasts for information about what to expect the next day.

"Nothing," Mom called back. "It's doing the best it can under the circumstances."

Jackson jumped up. "If we're walking to Hugo's for dinner, we should leave early and take our time. It's too hot to walk fast."

Suddenly, the air conditioner stopped, and the television went black. Jeff yelled from his bedroom. "Hey! The computer just died!"

Jackson peeked out the apartment door into the hallway. It had been hot out there. Now it was also dark—and strangely quiet. He got a flashlight and headed down the hall to the elevators. He put his ear to the closed door and heard the emergency buzzers.

A while later, Dad called on his cell phone. "Hugo's is closed, and the subways aren't running. I'm going to have to walk home!"

Mom sighed and wondered how long it would be before the food in the refrigerator would all have to be thrown out and how much it would cost to replace everything. At the same time, Jeff wondered how much of his history paper would be lost, too.

"Maybe the power will come back on soon," Grandma fretted as Jackson pulled candles from a drawer in the kitchen. "Candles can be so dangerous."

Then the cell phone rang again. It was Aunt

Agatha in Ohio, calling on her cell. She was stuck

between floors in an elevator in her office building.

But Aunt Agatha lived hundreds of miles away! What

was going on here?

Many families keep an emergency "survival kit." What might such a kit contain and why? What things besides medicines should be included?

CHAPTER THREE

MAKING AND DELIVERING ELECTRICITY

*The first widespread blackout in New York City and
other parts of the Northeast took place in 1965.*

The people in the story experienced a failure in the system that delivers electric power. In such a **blackout,** lights and everything else that runs on electricity stop working. The story deals with only a few problems that a power failure causes. What made this blackout special is that both Jackson's family in New York and his aunt in Ohio, hundreds of miles away, were affected by it.

The story pointed out the importance of electric power in our lives. Now let's look at how electric power is developed and supplied to the whole country. Let's also look at some real-life examples of what happens when the power fails.

Learning & Innovation Skills

What machine in your house uses electricity all day every day? *Hint:* Think about the kitchen.

To learn how and why a blackout happens, we need to understand **power grids**. These are the systems that make electrical power and then send that power where it is needed. Everything involved in this process is part of a power grid.

Electricity is produced in a **power plant** from particles called **atoms**. Everything you can think of, everything in the world, is made up of these particles. Atoms are so small that they can be seen only under a microscope.

Electric meters like this one measure the exact amount of electricity that is used in a home or other specific place.

An **electron** is one part of an atom. Each electron contains a small

amount of electrical energy. Scientists have learned to produce electric

power from electrons. It is necessary to run the world as we know it.

Most power plants generate electricity by burning coal, oil, or natural gas. From major power plants, electric power is sent to smaller plants, or **substations**. Substations are closer to where the power will be used. Power lines that carry the electricity go from the substations to tall metal towers. From those towers, electricity moves through a large power line to a smaller one and into a building. Then individual wiring systems take it to where it is needed.

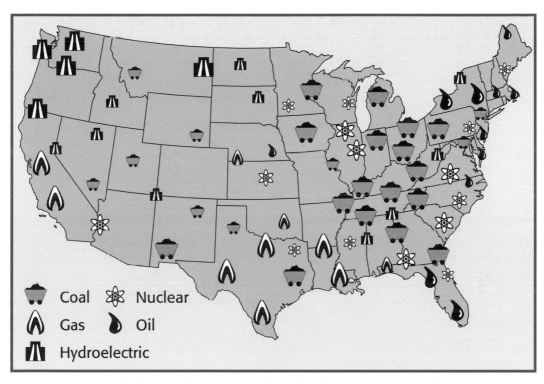

*Coal, natural gas, water, oil, and nuclear energy are used
to power America's electric plants.*

This map shows the types of energy sources used at the major power

stations in the United States. These energy sources include gas, coal, oil,

hydroelectric, and nuclear energy. Remember that each power station is

connected to dozens of substations, hundreds of towers, and thousands

of lines and poles.

CHAPTER FOUR

THE NATIONAL POWER GRID

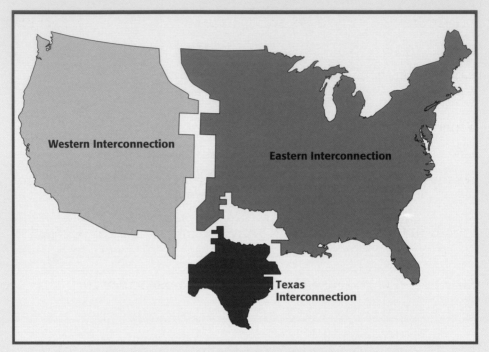

*Dispatch centers maintain and control the flow of electricity
over the grid and supply power to meet demand.*

The continental United States is divided into three huge electric grids.

(Alaska and Hawaii have their own separate systems.) The divisions are

the Eastern Interconnection, the Western Interconnection, and the Texas

Interconnection. They make up the National Power Grid.

The only place you can see these massive grids is on a map. When you are on the ground, you can see some of the smaller grids—a power plant here, a tall pole there—that are interconnected to make a large one.

When a smaller regional power grid operates on its own, it can draw only on its own resources. Connecting the smaller grids has given everybody in the system access to greater resources. This is especially important during periods of high demand in a particular area.

*The American Northeast is an area of severe snow and
ice storms that can bring down electric lines.*

For example, the interconnected resources of the entire Eastern Power Grid might supply a great deal of power to Alabama for a few months during a very hot summer.

Then, during a severe winter, grids in Florida might send power to cold New England states. However, once the grids are joined together, the failure of one can lead to the failure of them all.

Electricity can be very dangerous, so power plants are set to shut down in times of trouble. The shutdowns can prevent massive fires and other damage. But the shutdowns also cause people in that area to lose all electric power for a while.

CHAPTER FIVE

FAILURE! A REAL LIFE EXAMPLE

A blackout grows when a shower, or cascade, of problems causes more problems in other parts of the system. Then, each one of these new problems causes several more. This is what happened in 2003.

Major storms such as hurricanes or ice storms may require electric company workers from many nearby states to restore power.

Between 4:04 and 4:13 on the very hot afternoon on August 14, 2003, more than 250 power plants in the Eastern Interconnection shut down. Some 50 million people were suddenly without electric power. The power failure covered more than a million square miles.

New York, Cleveland, Toronto, Albany, Buffalo, Detroit, and other cities were without power. All the gas station pumps quit working. Railroad trains were halted because signals didn't work. Sewage pumps failed, and beaches were contaminated. Computers, TVs, and movie screens suddenly went dark. Garage door openers, ATMs, and stoplights quit working. Thousands of workers couldn't get home and slept in parks or in front of office buildings.

Some areas were without safe drinking water for days, and fires used to provide nighttime light got out of control and killed at least two people. The number of traffic accidents soared, as did health problems related to heat, activity, and stress. Emergency power supplies kept some hospitals open, but others had to cut back services or close. Twelve airports shut down, causing delays and cancellations across the country. Overall, the blackout cost billions of dollars.

Life & Career Skills

Think again about the things for your survival kit. Would you add anything else? If so, what?

Being without a cool place to stay and enough water to drink during a heat wave can be dangerous.

Some areas got back electricity relatively quickly while others were without power for days. Restarting a power station is much more complicated than turning on a lamp in the living room. Systems had to be checked and approved for service before power could be produced again. Thousands of workers were needed to do this, and they had to work methodically through thousands of steps before power could flow again.

CHAPTER SIX

PROTECTING THE GRID

Downed power lines interrupt power to homes and businesses.

How could such a thing happen? Investigators determined that the 2003

blackout began when one power station automatically shut down because

there was more demand for power than it could handle. Then, a power

line in another part of the Eastern grid was knocked down when a tree branch fell on it. The cascade had begun.

The 2003 blackout led to deaths, equipment destruction, huge costs, and discomfort. But it did teach us a valuable lesson. We learned how little it takes to bring the system crashing down around us.

In spite of its problems, our National Power Grid is one of the best in the world. However, investigators of the 2003 events stressed the need for more up-to-date computers and software.

Of equal importance is teaching employees how to best use the equipment. In 2003 for example, computer programs hinted that things were getting out of hand, but operators did not understand the signals.

All equipment also must be kept in good condition. This means inspecting power plants and keeping millions of miles of line and countless towers and poles in good repair. In 2003 in Ohio, smaller budgets had led to a reduction in tree trimming near power lines.

Maintaining power lines is a key task for electric power companies everywhere.

Protecting the grid from terrorists is very important. Even a small amount of explosives could do serious damage. Or terrorists might hack into power grid computers and cause a massive problem. Acts of vandalism such as starting fires or breaking equipment must also be prevented.

As a result, all power plants update security systems regularly and do detailed background checks on employees. Of course, complete security details are not released. Some of the best safeguards are ones the public is never told about.

It is almost impossible to exaggerate the importance of electricity and the power grid to our

*Reliable electric power has become a key part of
Americans' lives in the twenty-first century.*

lives. We need it to heat and cool our houses, power our factories, and run

our hospitals. We need it for play, for work, and for basic living. Keeping

the system up to date and safe is without question one of the major

challenges in our world.

Glossary

atom [AT-uhm] small amount of material, invisible to the naked eye, that contains the electrons from which electric power is made. Everything is made up of atoms.

blackout [BLAK-out] nickname for a power failure, referring to the loss of all lights

electron [i-LEK-tron] part of an atom that carries an electrical charge

power grid [POU-er grid] system through which electricity is produced and distributed throughout a region

power plant [POU-er plant] building containing the machinery used for making power

substations [SUBH-stey-shuhns] branch stations, which are smaller than a power plant

For More Information

Books

Aldrich, Lisa J. *Nicola Tesla and the Taming of Electricity.* Greensboro, NC: Morgan Reynolds Publishing, Inc., 2005.

Brunelle, Lynn. *Pop Bottle Science.* New York: Workman, 2004.

Cole, Joanna. *The Magic School Bus and the Electric Field Trip.* New York: Scholastic, 2004.

Frith, Margaret. *Who Was Thomas Alva Edison?* New York: Grosset & Dunlap, 2005.

Glover, David. *Batteries, Bulbs, and Wires.* New York: Kingfisher, 2002.

Graf, Rudolf F. *Safe and Simple Electrical Experiments.* New York: Dover, 1973.

Parker, Steve. *Electricity.* New York: Dorling Kindersley, 2005.

Other Media

Electric Nation. VHS. PBS Home Video, 2002.

Tesla: Master of Lightning. VHS. PBS Home Video.

Thomas A. Edison—Father of Invention. DVD. Biography Channel, 2006.

http://www.teachnet.ie/pcoakley/consumers.htm has more information about electricity and some activities to try.

INDEX

ABOUT THE AUTHOR

Patricia Hynes grew up in Pennsylvania, where she climbed hills and trees and swam in the local river. She attended college in Pennsylvania and got a degree in literature and secondary education. In both high school and college, her writing was published in school literary journals. She has spent her adult life teaching and writing for young people and has lived in Baltimore, Boston, Chicago, Florida, and Canada. She now lives in Venice, California, with her husband, a painter and dentist, and a fluffy orange cat named Stinky.